RENEWAL
— OF —
LIFE!

Photo By: Author

AVIS SIMMONDS

Print information available on the last page

Rev. date: 12/28/2018

To order additional copies of this book, contact:
Xlibris
1-888-795-4274
www.Xlibris.com
Orders@Xlibris.com

RENEWAL
— OF —
LIFE!

DEDICATION

I am fortunate to have an almost Two-year old granddaughter at my age of 67. I trust she will have wonderful experiences on the reflections of life as she grows and that she will have keen eyes for the renewal of life around her; cherishing and managing the phases of her life.

I thank my son, Kevin and my daughter-in-law, Parisha, for raising her to be a happy baby and that, that happiness continues into her adulthood.

I therefore dedicate this book to my granddaughter, Amaris L. Simmonds.

Avis Simmonds

December 2018

Hatching of the Bird's egg and the specie's life is renewed

"Give us this day our daily bread…"

Food nourishes and renews life

The birth of a newborn signifies the continuation of life and the renewal of the family genes

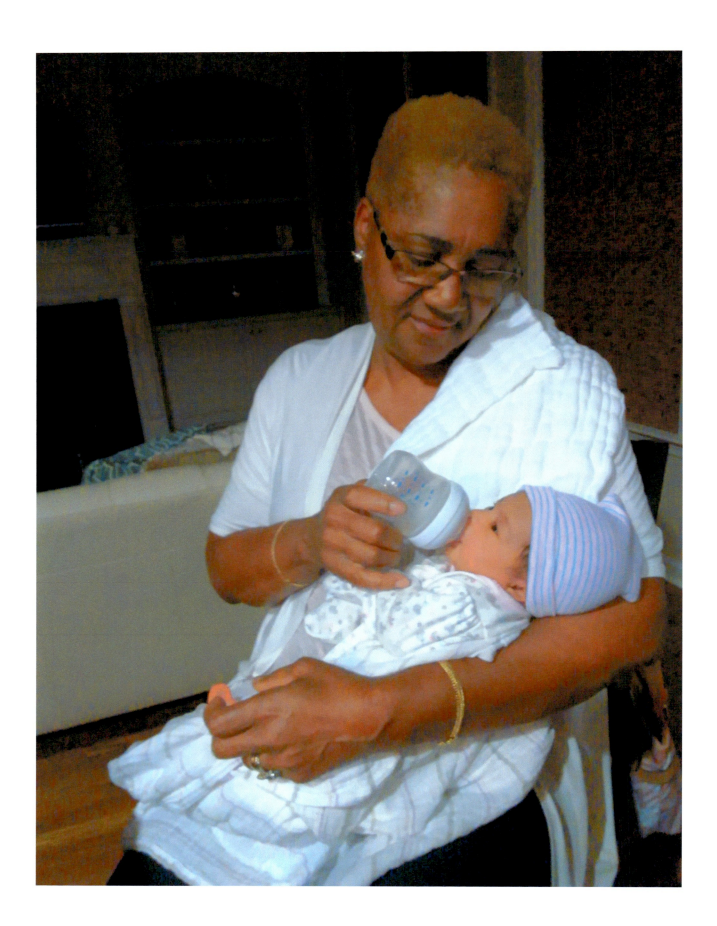

The imparting of knowledge, renews life

Springtime renews the plants' life

The flame of life!

Water not only cleanses, but renews life

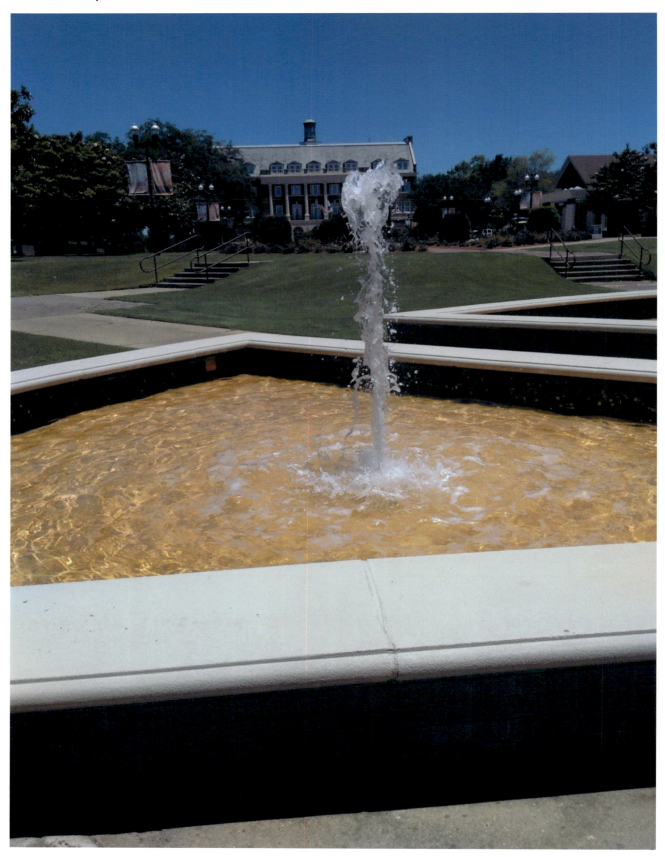

Drinking of water most definitely renews Life

Life is renewed even between the rocks

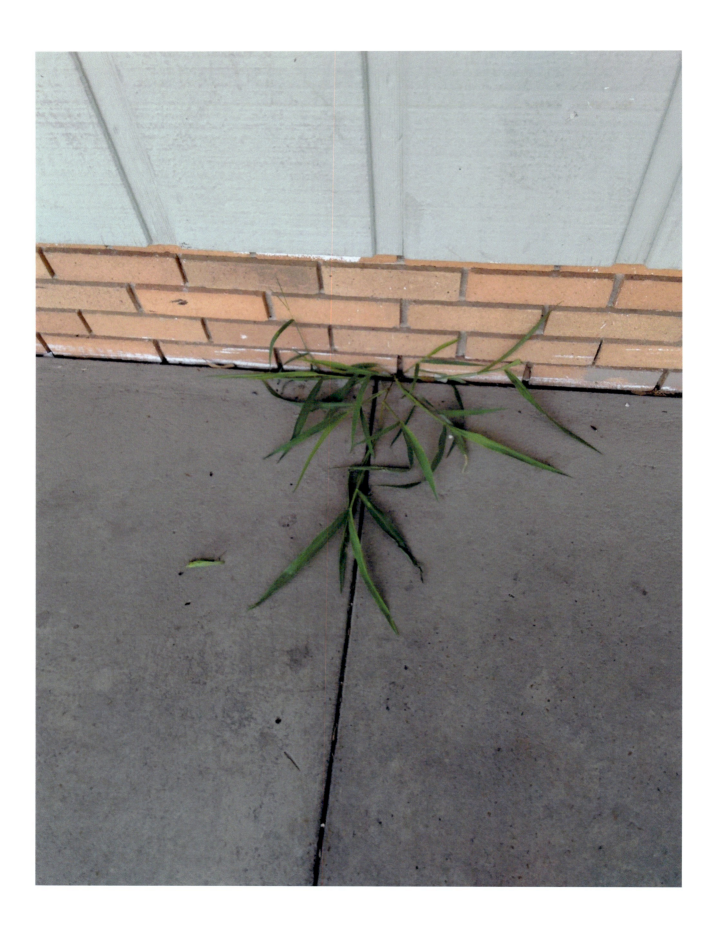

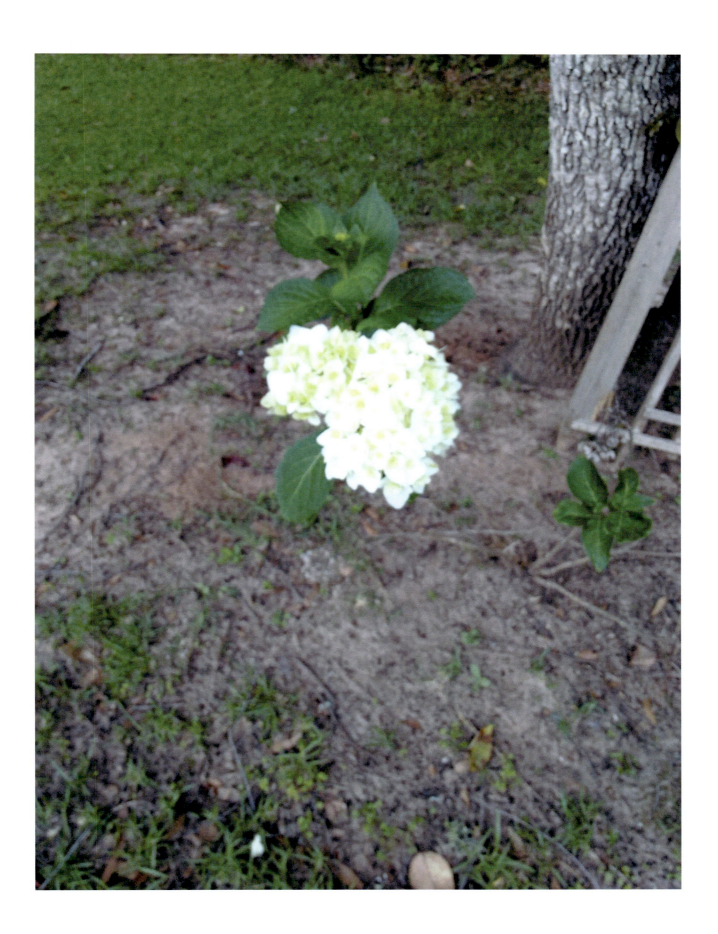

The blooming of the flowers depicts the renewal of the tree's life

River of Jordan Baptism, Israel May, 2013. Baptism Speaks to Renewal of one's religious faith in life

Medical Checkups Renews the quality of one's Life

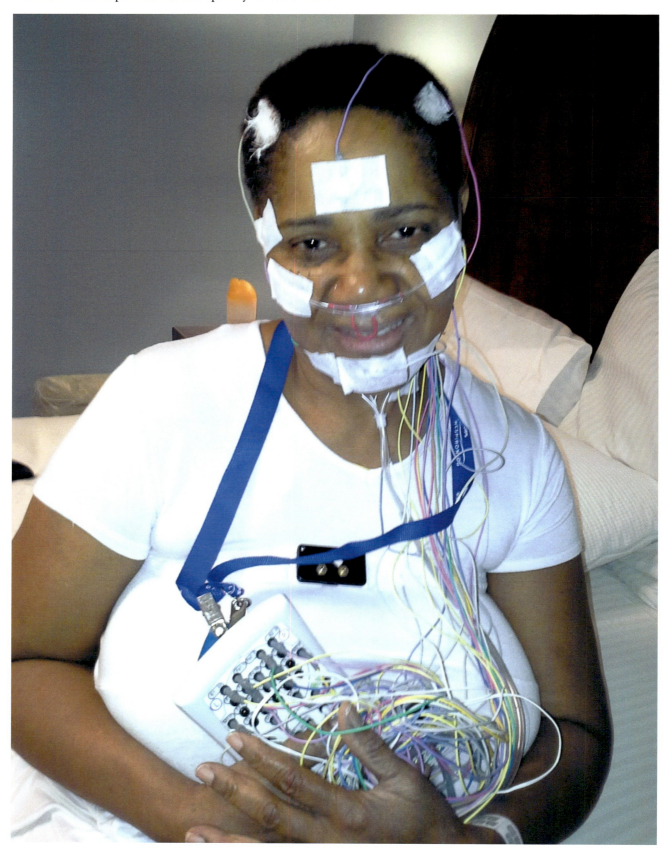

Vegetables for the renewal of Life!

A fish and a loaf will renew a life!

The Rainbow - promise of the renewal of life

The Fall Season

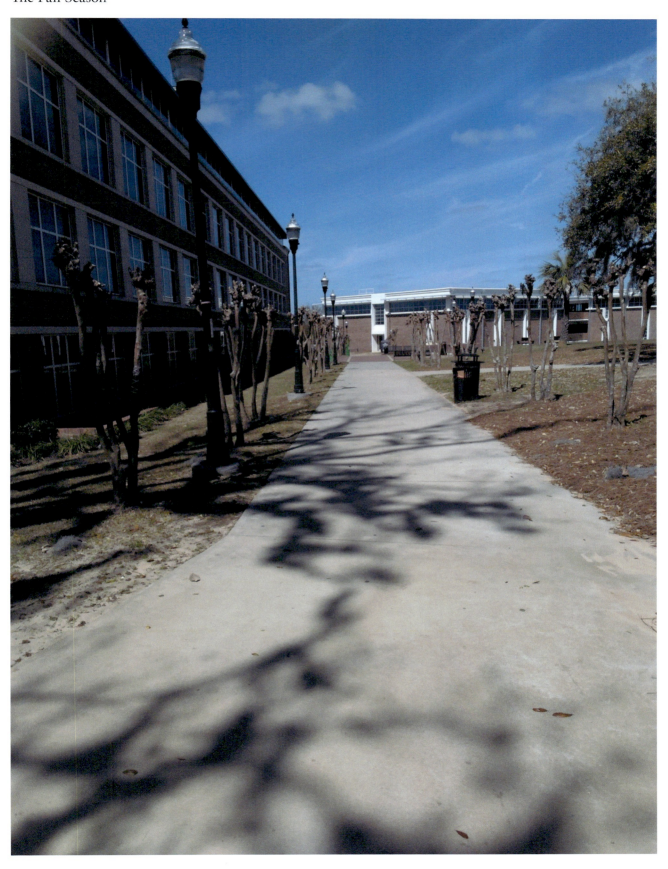

Spring Season Renews

Life is renewed in the unexpected places!

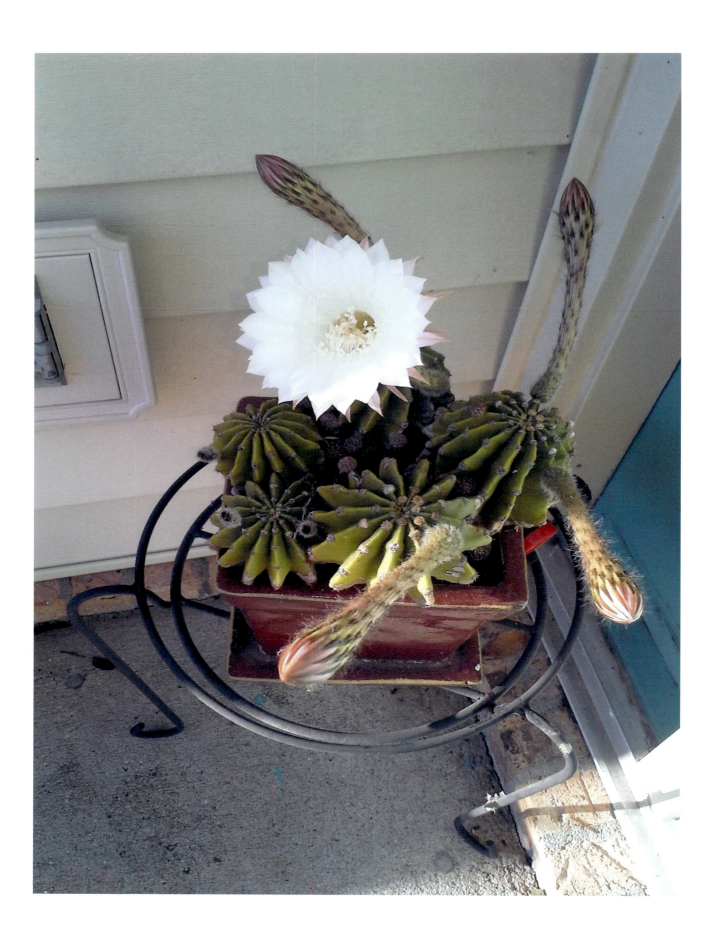

As I walked around the town, my eyes caught the shared photos in this book about life, and I thought, why not share these scenes of life's renewal. Because life is not just our daily waking up and going to work or about our designated business, life exists in places we do not easily observe because of our busy daily schedules. Therefore, take a moment and observe your surroundings; you might be able to breath easily in your haste to reach your next destination. Enjoy the Now of life!

Avis Veronica Simmonds

Printed in the United States
By Bookmasters